On the 8th day...

GOD

Laughed!

Gene Perret
with Terry Perret Martin

To Tina + Chris
Have some laughter
Be(Always
[signature]

To Tina + Chris~
Hope this helps
keeps you
laughing +
praying!
Terry

Copyright Gene Perret & Terry Perret Martin
FIRST EDITION PRINTED APRIL, 1995
ISBN 0-929292-81-2
Library of Congress 95-076070

Printed in the United States of America by Lithocolor Press, Inc.
Cover by Cyndi Allison
(Use coupons in back to order extra copies of this and
other books from Hannibal Books)

For Mary

* * * * *

*To Mom and Dad for my love of
God and humor*

AUTHORS' FOREWORD

God created the world, and us, in six days. On the seventh day, He rested, but we believe that there was an eighth day when He sat back and had a good, hearty laugh.

Let's face it, we are laughable. Those who don't believe that should take a good look around at the next cousin's picnic, install a full length mirror in the bathroom, or just listen to some of the answers they give while watching "Jeopardy."

This life has sometimes been described as "a vale of tears," and it can be that, but it's also mercifully offset by God's gift to us of laughter.

This is not a gift God just drops in our laps. It's one He shares with us. Laughter is so much more enjoyable when it's shared with a friend.

If any one word describes our relationship with God and His relationship with us, it's "joy." What can be more joyous than a big belly laugh?

We'll smile, chuckle, giggle, and guffaw in Heaven, so why not start now?

The lines in this book are not here to *make* fun, but to *have* fun.

Enjoy.

Gene Perret
Terry Perret Martin

Table of Contents

ADAM AND EVE

1   Where would we be today if Adam and Eve believed in zero population growth?

2   Adam and Eve were the first two people on earth. All the rest of us are descended from them. They formed the world's first and only successful Pyramid Club.

3   It was Eve who first said to Adam, "You're the reason we have no friends."

4   Adam and Eve had many advantages, but the principal one was that they escaped teething.

☞Mark Twain

5   With Adam and Eve, it was love at first sight. There was no one else to look at.

6   When Adam said, "I'm seeing someone else," it was his eyesight that was going bad, not his marriage.

7   One bad thing about being Adam and Eve — very few wedding gifts.

8   Of course, Adam and Eve weren't really married. Couldn't get witnesses.

9   Adam and Eve didn't hit it off initially. When he first proposed she said, "I wouldn't marry you if you were the first man on earth."

10   Adam invented love at first sight, one of the greatest labor saving devices the world ever saw.

☞Josh Billings

11   Adam and Eve were lucky. No matter where they went they were first in line.

12   Adam and Eve always celebrated New Years Eve at home. He hated crowds.

13　Adam and Eve had a perfect life in the Garden of Eden. No traffic.

14　Adam was luckier than he ever realized. He had a marriage with no mother-in-law.

15　What a good thing Adam had — when he said "a good thing" he knew nobody had said it before.

☞Mark Twain

16　You want to talk about useless items? How about Adam and Eve hanging a "do not disturb" sign on the door of their honeymoon suite?

17　Eve said, "Adam, how come you never take me anywhere?" He said, "Can't find a baby sitter."

18　Eve said she wanted to move. Adam said, "No, I like it in the Garden of Eden." Eve said, "Let's go have an apple and talk it over."

---

19   Adam was tired of living alone and he said to the Lord, "I'd like a companion. I want the perfect creature who will care for me and comfort me and be there whenever I need solace."

The Lord said, "OK, but it'll cost you an arm and a leg."

Adam replied, "What can I get for just a rib?"

---

20   Adam and Eve committed the original sin. They had to; there was no one else there.

---

21   The bad news is that we all inherited the consequences of the first sin. The good news is that there's no inheritance tax.

---

22   An angel escorted Adam and Eve out of the Garden of Eden. How do you like that? A bouncer with wings.

---

23   The worst part of Adam and Eve being cast out of the Garden of Eden is that since they were the only people on earth — they had no friends to come over to help them with the move.

24   Adam and Eve were the only people on earth. As he cast them out of the Garden of Eden, the angel was heard to mutter to himself, "Well, there goes the neighborhood."

AGNOSTICS

25   An agnostic is an atheist who likes to hedge his bets.

26   Somebody found out I was an agnostic, so he burned a question mark on my lawn.

☞Milton Berle

27   An agnostic is not sure whether there's a God or not. When he gets to the Pearly Gates, St. Peter might say, "I'm not sure whether I'm going to let you in or not."

28 If only God would give me a clear sign. Like a large deposit in my name at a Swiss bank.

☞Woody Allen

29 An agnostic is not only wishy-washy, but can't even decide whether he wants to be more wishy or more washy.

30 An agnostic is someone who might say his prayers but instead of "amen" at the end, he says, "maybe."

31 An agnostic can't fold his hands in prayer because he's too busy scratching his head in confusion.

32 The Lord said, "If you're not with Me, you're against Me." And the agnostic says, "I'm not even sure who's talking."

33 Agnostics are befuddled. They're like a religious version of "Who's on first?"

34 The agnostic's prayer:
Now I lay me down to sleep,
And pray someone my soul to keep.
If I should die before I wake,
Maybe I'll finally get some definitive answers.

35 Agnosticism is neither here nor there. It's like taking a shower with your raincoat on.

It's like trying to buy a lottery ticket on time.

36 Agnostics say, "I don't know if there is a God. I haven't made up my mind yet." God says, "Take your time. You've got all eternity."

37 You can always spot an agnostic's funeral. Three pallbearers are facing one way and three are facing the other way.

38   If agnosticism were mathematics, we would all be taught that 2 plus 2 are something, but we're not sure what.

39   The beginning of the agnostic's Lord's Prayer defends their philosophy: "Our Father, who may or may not dwell in Heaven…"

40   Eternal nothingness is okay if you're dressed for it.

☞Woody Allen

41   Agnostics have to accept some things on faith; otherwise, they'd never allow a dentist near their mouths with a long needle and a drill.

ANGELS

42   You know what must really be tough? To be an angel who's afraid of heights and can't stand harp music.

43   My mom once told me that you could get 10,000 angels on the head of a pin. I said, "What do you do with them once you got them there?"

---

44 The Sunday school teacher told her students that you could get 10,000 angels on the head of a pin. One enterprising young student said, "Great, now if we could only figure out a way to charge admission."

---

45 The Sunday school teacher told her students that angels can fly anywhere they want. One youngster raised his hand and asked, "Are they limited to two pieces of carry-on luggage?"

46

My dad said he didn't believe in angels because they could go anywhere they wanted just by thinking about that place. He said, "It's silly. They expect us to believe that angels have wings but they can't fly."

I said, "It's not so silly. You have golf clubs."

47 Angels can go anywhere just by thinking about it. That's very convenient, but they're missing out on a lot of frequent flyer bonuses.

...to say nothing of all those honey roasted peanuts.

48 A wife told her husband, "Be an angel and let me drive." He did and he is.

☞Milton Berle

49 I believe angels can perform miracles. They have to. It's the only way they can get their T-shirts on and off over their wings.

50 All angels have wings, so I wouldn't try to become one if you like to sleep on your back.

51 Angels have always been God's messengers. It makes you wonder if they might not be replaced with the invention of the fax machine.

52 When the Angel Gabriel blows his horn at the end of the world, he will wake up all the dead people from their graves. The kid next door to me takes trumpet lessons. He plays so badly he can almost wake the dead right now.

53 Two religious youngsters were overheard fighting in the schoolyard: "Oh yeah? Well, my guardian angel can beat up your guardian angel."

ATHEISTS

54 Nobody talks so consistently about God as those who insist there is no God.

☞Heywood Broun

55 I knew a gentleman who said, "If the Good Lord's willing, I'll be an atheist for the rest of my life."

56 One gentleman likes to go to wakes for atheists. He said, "I like to see them fellas all dressed up with no place to go."

57   Once I wanted to be an atheist, but I gave it up. They have no holidays.

☞Henny Youngman

58   If you stick your finger into an electrical outlet, it's going to knock your socks off — whether you believe in electricity or not.

59   Maybe you heard about the dyslexic atheist? He said, "I don't believe in dog."

60   A preacher was trying to witness to a certain gentleman. The man said, "Save your breath, Reverend. I'm an atheist." The preacher said, "I'm sorry, but I don't believe in atheists."

61   She was an atheist and I was an agnostic. We didn't know what religion not to bring the children up in.

☞Woody Allen

62 One very influential atheist died and got to the Pearly Gates. St. Peter wouldn't admit him. The man argued and cajoled, but St. Peter wouldn't give in. Finally, the man said, "I'm not used to dealing with underlings. I want to talk to God Himself."

St. Peter went to his book, flipped the pages and searched for some time, then said, "You know something? You atheists must have been right. We don't have anybody up here by that name."

63 An atheist was out fishing when he was suddenly attacked by the Loch Ness monster. It was 160 feet long, breathed fire, had sharp teeth and claws like an eagle. It crushed the boat, grabbed the man, and was about to eat him. The man prayed, "Please, God, help me."

A voice from Heaven said, "I thought you didn't believe there was a God."

The man said, "Right, and I didn't believe there was a Loch Ness monster either."

64   I did meet an honest atheist once. He said, "I'd believe in God if they held church services a little later on Sunday mornings."

65   They now have a special Dial-A-Prayer number for atheists. You call it and nobody answers.

☞Milton Berle

66   An atheist died and went to Heaven. He met God and said, "I never believed in You, but now I'd like to say hello."

God said, "Make that hello and goodbye."

67   An atheist died and went to his judgment. When he met God he said, "I hate to tell You this, but I never thought You existed."

God said, "I hate to tell you this, but I do."

68   One day a preacher said to a group, "Let's all bow our heads in prayer." One man took exception to that and said loudly and proudly, "I am an atheist." The preacher said, "Then you can bow your head in confusion."

69   Definition of an atheist: A guy who doesn't care if SMU or Notre Dame wins the football game.

☞Woody Woodbury

70   One atheist refused to change his beliefs until the end. As he was dying he shouted, "I'm going to Disneyland."

71   One man gave up atheism when he took up golf. He said, "When you hit the ball like I do you've got to have someone to pray to."

72   One atheist arrived at the Pearly Gates. He rang the bell and a loud voice said, "There's nobody home."

73   One atheist died and kept banging on the entrance to Heaven. Finally he shouted, "God, are You in there?" God shouted back, "Yes, and you're not."

74   Our pastor asked one atheist, "If there is no God then where did we get the trees and the sun and the moon and the stars?" The man replied, "Home Shopping Club?"

75   One atheist refused to believe there was a God until he was struck by lightning. It changed his life. Now he believes in God during thunder storms.

76   One man proclaimed, "I'm an atheist and nothing God can do will ever change that."

77   I asked one man why he was an atheist. He said, "Fewer commandments."

78 I don't believe in the hereafter. If you don't get it here, you won't get it after.

☞Max Asnas

BIBLE CHARACTERS

79 Methuselah lived to be over 900 years old. He had the world's largest collection of humorous birthday cards.

...The last three years of his life were spent blowing out the candles on his birthday cake.

80 Methuselah eventually died of boredom. He couldn't meet any women his age.

81 Methuselah lived to be over 900 years old. That means he got senior discount prices for over 835 years.

82 Methuselah got so old his skin turned to parchment.

83 Jonah lived for three days in the belly of the whale. It was just him and two antacid tablets.

84 "Jonah" in fish language means "heartburn."

85 Jonah would say his prayers each night "Lord keep me away from harm in the belly of the whale, and keep the whale away from Captain Ahab for a few days, too."

86 They asked Moses why there were three commandments on one tablet and seven on the other. Moses said, "After the first tablet, I learned to write smaller."

87 One Sunday school student thought Moses was a gangster because his brother Aaron carried a rod.

88 After 20 years in the wilderness, Aaron finally found the courage to ask

Moses why the birds always flew upside-down.

"Because the scenery is better," was his reply.

---

89 Moses led his people through the desert for 40 years. You've got to love sand to stay in that group.

…You'd think someone would have said, "Hey, let me take a look at that road map for a minute."

---

90 If Goliath lost to David nowadays, he'd be on Wide World of Sports each week as "The Agony of Defeat."

---

91 The year after David defeated Goliath, the Philistines tried to get the rules committee to outlaw slingshots.

---

92 Lot never enjoyed home cooking. Everything his wife cooked had too much salt in it.

---

93 Poor Job had a rough time in the Bible. He lost everything he had, including his nickname, "Lucky."

94   Job was the original embodiment of a Joe E. Lewis nightclub line: "I've been rich and I've been poor. Rich is better."

95   I'm always on a diet. If I'd come down from Mount Sinai instead of Moses, the two tablets would have been saccharin.

☞Milton Berle

BLESSED ARE ...

96   Blessed are the meek for they shall inherit the earth — if there's anything left when we get done with it.

97   The first thing the meek will do when they inherit the earth is hire some strong guys to protect them from losing it.

☞Milton Berle

98   Blessed are the meek for they'll always let us get in line ahead of them.

99   Blessed are the meek for they shall inherit the earth — and then get stuck with all the taxes.

100 The meek shall inherit the earth. They won't have the nerve to refuse it.

☞Jackie Vernon

101 It is going to be fun to watch and see how long the meek can keep the earth after they inherit it.

☞Kin Hubbard

102 Blessed are the peacemakers, although they'll never get to referee a hockey game.

103 Blessed are the peacemakers. We couldn't have a family picnic without them.

104 Blessed are the pure of heart even though there are very few movies they can go to today.

105 Blessed are the pure of heart —
all half a dozen or so of them.

106 Blessed are those who hunger and
thirst. Without them there'd be no
concession stands at the ball park.

CHURCH SINGING

107 We had a guy in our church who
sang so badly, if there were an eleventh
commandment, he would have been
mentioned in it by name.

...It would have been "Hey, Mr.
McGillicudy, thou shalt not sing."

108 The preacher would say,
"Everyone turn to page 37 in your
hymnals, except for you, Mr.
McGillicudy. You turn to the window
that's been boarded up."

109 We always invited him to sing at
the church picnic. It kept most of the
ants away ... all but the deaf ones.

110 He had a very biblical voice. He sounded like the whale ... while he was swallowing Jonah.

111 Our preacher said the Lord liked Mr. McGillicudy's singing. Which leads me to believe that Heaven must have at least one sound proof room.

112 One lady in our church had a real high pitched voice. She could hit a high note that could open a pickle jar.

113 When she left church there'd be a whole bunch of dogs outside just waiting to get her autograph.

114 When she hit a high note even the statues put their hands over their ears.

115 We even had some people in town who tried to have her banned from singing on Sundays. It was mostly the store owners who had plate glass windows.

116 She had a real biblical voice, too. She could have brought down the walls of Jericho and parted the Red Sea all with the same note.

117 She sang in church — and fifty people changed religions.

☞Joey Adams

CLEANLINESS IS NEXT TO GODLINESS

118 My mother believed that cleanliness was next to Godliness. She used to keep my brothers and me so clean we always thought we were for sale.

119 Mom would always tell me to wash behind my ears... wash behind my ears. It used to make me wonder what was going on back there that was getting them so dirty.

120 I used to keep behind my ears so clean that by comparison the rest of me seemed dirty.

121 My mom made me wash up before doing anything. We kids used to have to wash up before taking a bath.

122 I spent half my childhood washing up. I would have spent less time around water if I had been born a goldfish.

123 Heck, I used to have to wash up before changing my mind.

124 Mom kept everything spotless. Furniture in our house had to go outside to get dusty.

125 I hope St. Peter keeps Heaven sparkling clean, because if he doesn't my mom ain't going in.

    She's not going to spend eternity anyplace that has dustballs under the throne.

126 My mom starched everything. My brother knelt down to say his prayers one night and cracked his pajamas.

He sneezed one time and cut his nose on his handkerchief.

127 Mom loved starch. I used to have to put my socks on with a shoehorn.

128 Mom starched everything. You try going through your childhood wearing plywood underwear.

129 My mom put so much starch in my longjohns that I had to carry around a crowbar to open the flap in the back.

130 I was the laughing stock of the playground one day when the other kids found out that Mom starched the string on my yo-yo.

131 Go, and never darken my towels again.

☞Groucho Marx

132 I finally found out how my neighbor — whom I call Mrs. Clean — gets her laundry so much whiter looking than mine. She washes it.

☞Phyllis Diller

133 Have I got a mother-in-law. She's so neat she puts paper under the cuckoo clock.

☞Henny Youngman

134 Fang is very good about putting out the garbage. Sometimes he doesn't even wait till I serve it.

☞Phyllis Diller

135 She's an expert housekeeper. Every time she gets divorced, she keeps the house.

☞Henny Youngman

COLLECTIONS

136 My church takes all denominations — tens, twenties, fifties.

☞Milton Berle

137 Our preacher prayed, "Dear God, I ask you to inspire the people in this church to give until it hurts." Instead of "Amen," the entire congregation responded with "Ouch."

138 The preacher said, "Please be generous when the collection plate is passed today and remember, the longer it takes me to count the money, the shorter my sermon will be next Sunday."

The congregation was generous since it was for such a good cause.

139 Our preacher said, "Brethren, I need your financial support in my work. The best things in life are free, but I'm not one of them."

140 "I advertised that the poor would be welcome in this church," said the minister, "and after inspecting the collection, I see that they have come."

☞ Joey Adams

141 The preacher spoke for an hour and a half about how the congregation must support the church financially, how people had to be more generous in subsidizing the Lord's work, how they must contribute joyfully to this mission.

"People will gladly pay $100 to see a Broadway show," he said. "Why?"

Someone was heard to whisper, "They have intermission."

142 The preacher said, "Do you believe the Lord's word?" The congregation said, "We do believe the Lord's word." The Preacher said, "Do you believe in spreading the Lord's word?" The congregation said, "We do believe in spreading the Lord's word." The Preacher said, "Will you double your contributions to support us in spreading the Lord's word?" The congregation said, "Two out of three's not bad."

143 A gentleman was flying on a plane that experienced quite a bit of turbulence. He got frightened and prayed. He said aloud, "Lord, I'm a rich man. If you let this plane land safely, I promise to give You half of everything I own."

The plane landed safely and this man was the first one off. As he was hurrying through the terminal someone tapped him on the shoulder and said, "Excuse me, sir, but I was on that plane with you. I heard what you said. You said if the Lord would let the plane land safely, you'd give Him half of everything you own. Well, I'm a man of the cloth and I'm here to collect."

The man said, "No, I made the Lord a better offer. I told Him if He ever catches me on another plane again, He can have it *all*."

---

144 A gentleman was on a plane that was in serious trouble. Someone onboard the plane suggested that all the passengers bow their heads in prayer. One man didn't. Others asked why. He said, "I don't believe in prayer." They said, "Well, do something religious." He took up a collection.

145 The preacher said, "The Lord loves a cheerful giver. Me — I like a giver even if he has the personality of a piranha."

146 I took up a collection for a man in our office. But I didn't get enough money to buy one.

☞Ruth Buzzi

147 They took up so many collections at the office where I worked that for the first three months I worked there I genuflected.

CONSCIENCE

148 Conscience: It takes up more room than all the rest of a person's insides.

☞Mark Twain

149 As a kid, my mom had me convinced that conscience was a good angel who sat on my right shoulder and ruined a lot of my fun.

150 According to my conscience everything is either sinful, illegal, or fattening.

151 If you're going to do something tonight that you'll be sorry for tomorrow morning — sleep late.

☞Henny Youngman

152 Lately it seems that whatever my conscience will allow, Weight Watchers won't.

153 My conscience used to tell me what I could and could not do. Now my arthritis does.

154 You've heard the expression "Eat, drink, and be merry...?" Well, conscience's motto is "Starve, stay thirsty, and try to make the best of it..."

155 Conscience is something that will tell you what's right and what's wrong

— so will the driver next to you on the freeway.

---

156 Conscience is the original "party pooper."

---

157 A conscience cannot prevent sin. It only prevents you from enjoying it.

☞Harry Hershfield

---

158 Conscience is the inner voice that whispers "someone may be looking."

☞H. L. Mencken

---

159 For most of us, when you come to a fork in the road, conscience will tell you you should have taken the other one.

---

160 Conscience tells you to always do the right thing. My daddy had a big long stick that did about the same thing.

---

161 My mom told me that conscience was a little voice inside me that would take me to Heaven. My Uncle Slurbo had little voices inside of him and they took him to the Funny Farm.

...Of course, his voices told him to run naked down Oak Street.

...At least, that's what he heard them say.

---

162 There's a devil on your left shoulder telling you the wrong things to do and an angel on your right shoulder telling you the right things to do. I have to admit there have been times in my life when that angel on my right shoulder must have come down with a case of laryngitis or something.

---

163 Conscience is a mother-in-law whose visit never ends.

☞H. L. Mencken

CREATION

164 Man was made at the end of a week's work when God was tired.

☞Mark Twain

165 God made the world in six days and on the seventh day He rested. Then on the eighth day — God laughed.

166 God made the entire world in six days, but remember that was before unions.

He could have made it in five, but He needed the overtime.

167 God took six days to complete the world. But that was in the days before building codes.

☞Milton Berle

168 God made the world in six days and on the seventh day He watched football on television.

169 God made the world in six days and on the seventh day He rested. Once He created man, He knew He wasn't going to get much rest after that.

170 God not only made the entire universe, but He did the whole thing without using nails or screws of any kind.

...He didn't even use duct tape!

171 God created the world as kind of a hobby. So we're lucky. This whole thing could have been made out of toothpicks.

172 God made the world in six days and on the seventh day He rested. Some people wished He had used that extra day to make the whole thing earthquake proof.

173 Do you realize it only took six days to create the world? Shows what can be done when you don't take coffee breaks.

☞Henny Youngman

174 I don't believe in the "Big Bang" theory of creation. Who would have been there to hear it?

175 God made man from a lump of clay. Some of us have not turned out to be that much of an improvement.

176 My theory of evolution? I think Darwin was adopted.

☞Steven Wright

177 God looked at what He created and it was beautiful. Of course it was — there was no one there yet to mess it up with grafitti.

178 God made a whole world of lush green grass and vegetation. Then He created man so He wouldn't have to do all the mowing Himself.

179 What if everything is an illusion and nothing exists? In that case, I definitely overpaid for my carpet.

☞Woody Allen

180 God created the world a long time ago. If He created it today, it probably would come with "some assembly required" and "batteries not included."

---

181 I don't think any schedule has ever been met. God made the world in six days, but he promised it in four.

DAY OF REST

182 I'm all for that day of rest. It's those six days that come before it that irritate me.

---

183 My day of rest is Sunday and any day when the boss is out of the office.

---

184 Sunday is the day when most of us bow our heads. Some of us praying and the rest of us playing golf.

☞Milton Berle

---

185 I have a friend who's a workaholic. His day of rest is February 30.
...and even then, only if it falls on a weekend.

186 I know a guy who has four young kids. He complains that his day of rest tires him out.

187 What puzzles me is when did my day of rest turn into my day of mowing the lawn and fixing the plumbing?

188 My wife says the only true day of rest is one where the meals cook themselves and the dishes wash each other.

189 Sunday is the traditional day of rest, but I must confess I sneak a little nap in from Monday to Friday, too.

190 For those who enjoy their day of rest too much, Monday becomes the day of atonement.

191 My Uncle Gribble takes his day of rest any day of the week that has a "y" in it.

192 Anyone who calls Sunday their day of rest has a lawn that grows much slower than mine does.

193 I go to church every Sunday — and pray for the strength to face next Monday to Friday.

194 I always like to get my beauty rest, but there are those who say that, for me, one day a week is not enough.

195 On the seventh day God rested — and I know He was in much better shape than I am.

196 If God really wanted Sunday to be our day of rest, He would have had church services start much later in the day.

DEVIL

197 They say that idle hands are the devil's workshop. That's one of the drawbacks of becoming a soccer player.

198 They say that idle hands are the devil's workshop. That's why you're going to see a lot of jugglers in Heaven.

199 The devil has two horns, a tail, red skin and a pitchfork. Not always easy to spot in a crowd.

...Sometimes he disguises himself as a good time.

200 I'm not sure I've ever seen the devil, but I'm pretty sure I've spent a couple of weekends with him.

201 I like to believe the devil is real. I'd hate to think that some of the things I've done in this life I thought of on my own.

202 They say the devil is evil, violent, and remorseless. A lot like one of today's hit movies.

203 Some people say that alcohol is the devil in a bottle. I believe it. I think I've choked on his tail a few times ... and woke up with that pitchfork still in my mouth the next morning.

---

204 I've seen the devil several times. He's usually driving that car that cuts me off on the highway.

...I've never spoken to him, but we have exchanged sign language.

---

205 I dreamed the devil appeared the other night and wanted to make a bargain for my soul and my agent handled the deal. He got me damned to Hell for eternity — with options.

☞Woody Allen

EXORCISM

206 Aunt Melva found out that exorcism meant chasing several demons out of the body. Now she wants to have it done. She'll try anything to lose weight.

---

207 The devil sometimes possesses people's bodies. He's welcome to Uncle Deebil's. He hardly ever uses his.

208 It's hard to get the devil out once you let him in. He's like visiting relatives.

209 I saw that movie, "The Exorcist." It scared the devil out of me.

210 A heretic is someone who went to see "The Exorcist" and rooted for the devil.

211 My mom used to say weird prayers over me when she thought I was tempted. It not only chased the devil away, but quite a few of my dates.

My mom chased so many devils away one year, I never did get a date for the senior prom.

212 My Uncle Finnel used to get possessed by demons occasionally, but he didn't need exorcism. He'd just sleep it off over the weekend.

FAITH, HOPE, AND CHARITY

213 Faith is believing in things you don't understand — like the first 4 or 5 pages of your tax return.

Charity is giving money away — like you do on the first 4 or 5 pages of your tax return.

Hope is trusting that the IRS will believe the first 4 or 5 pages of your tax return.

---

214 Faith is believing what you know ain't so.

☞Mark Twain

---

215 You can't get far ridiculing a man for upholding the Bible, or even the dictionary if it's his sincere belief.

☞Will Rogers

---

216 Faith is what it takes to eat someone else's tuna surprise.

Hope is that the "surprise" isn't what you think it is.

217 If there was no faith there would be no living in this world. We couldn't even eat hash with any safety.

☞Josh Billings

218 And how can I believe in God when just last week I got my tongue caught in the roller of my electric typewriter?

☞Woody Allen

219 If it weren't for hope, none of us could ever set the timer on our VCR.

220 Hope is what the bride's mother feels toward the groom.

Charity is what the bride's father will be giving to the bride and groom for a few years.

221 Charity is *giving* money to those in need — or *lending* money to a relative.

222 When we were first married we lived in a house so rundown once when I left a box of clothing on the front porch for the Good Will charity, they took the house too.

☞Phyllis Diller

223 I went to a celebrity charity ball ... I was the only one there I never heard of.

☞Henny Youngman

224 "Charity begins at home" is just a polite way of saying, "I got mine; you get yours."

225 Faith is when you believe in something even when the hard evidence doesn't prove it irrefutably, like believing in a Supreme Being, an afterlife, or that the new diet you're starting will finally be the one to work for you.

Hope is believing that everything will turn out the way you'd like it to, including that new diet you're starting.

Charity is when your friends say to you after three or four weeks of the new diet, "You've taken off a few pounds, haven't you?"

226 If it weren't for either faith, hope, or charity, no politician would ever get a vote.

227 Faith, Hope, and Charity — I had to call on all three to get a date for the senior prom.

FIRE AND BRIMSTONE

228 Our preacher taught fire and brimstone for so long that I asked to be buried in an asbestos suit.

229 I'm going to lead a good life. The fires of Hell don't scare me so much, but I think I'm allergic to brimstone.

...I'd hate to go through eternity with a runny nose.

230 The fires of Hell aren't going to get me. I've asked all my pallbearers to bring along a fire extinguisher.

231 We had a real fire and brimstone preacher. His sermons could leave you with blisters.

232 Our preacher used fire and brimstone as a fund raiser. He'd preach about how hot Hell was going to be and then made a fortune selling cold lemonade after the service.

233 Our preacher could make Hell sound so uncomfortable that even Satan would want to leave ... and he's the owner.

234 Fire and brimstone used to scare me, but not since they've come out with more powerful sunscreens.

235 I don't want to spend eternity in fire and brimstone. Heck, I got a nasty burn just spending two weeks in Hawaii.

...but I imagine Hell will be cheaper.

...except maybe for the gift shop.

FORGIVENESS

236 Always forgive your enemies — nothing annoys them so much.

☞Oscar Wilde

237 We've been told to forgive 70 times 7 times. Just forgive all the time. It's easier than doing the math.

238 To err is human
To forgive is divine
Especially when the sin to be forgiven
Is mine.

239 To err is human, to forgive supine.

☞S. J. Perelman

240 Have you noticed? The Good Lord is very good at forgiving and we're very good at requiring it.

241 Each day we pray for forgiveness. You'd think just one day we could go without needing it.

242 The minister asked, "What must we do before we can expect forgiveness of sin?"

A teenager in the front row said, "Sin!"

☞Milton Berle

243 I can forgive all trespasses, but there are some I just can't forget. Unfortunately, I can't remember which ones they are.

244 Forgiving and forgetting is not easy. I have a good friend who still can't forget the Alamo.

...He forgets his own zip code, but he can't forget the Alamo.

245 I asked my friend for forgiveness and he granted it immediately and unconditionally. I'll never forgive him for that.

246 Our God forgives all things. Boy, did we luck out.

247 I gave a talk to a bunch of priests once. They didn't pay me. They forgave me.

☞Henny Youngman

248 Have you ever noticed? It's easier to forgive a rich uncle than a poor nephew.

FREE WILL

249 I say enjoy your free will while it's still free … and before the government finds a way to tax it.

250 I don't know why they call it "free will." Everytime I use mine wrongly, it costs me.

251 When I was a kid, my mom told me I had a free will but she'd decide when and how I used it.

252 My brother used his free will very wisely. When he did good things, it was of his own free will; when he did bad things, he told Mom I did them.

---

253 Everybody has either a free will or an older brother who's a bully.

---

254 My Uncle Fenster says he used to have a free will, but he gave it up when he married Aunt Glinda.

"Well," he says, "I didn't exactly give it up. She took it."

---

255 Aunt Glinda says Uncle Fenster better have a free will because with the money he makes, that's the only kind they can afford.

---

256 Yogi Berra may have had the best explanation of free will "When you come to a fork in the road, take it."

---

257 We all have a free will. I just wish someone had told my sergeant in the Army about it.

258 I've often wondered which takes precedence — free will or a "Thank You For Not Smoking" sign.

259 Perhaps we all should have been born with a warning sign: "Caution, free will at work."

260 I was born with a free will but I was 26 years old before my mother would let me use it.

I didn't feel bad. She *never* did let Dad use his.

FUNERALS

261 Definition of a hypocrite: A mortician who tries to look sad at a $7000 funeral.

☞Woody Woodbury

262 When Lazarus returned from the dead, I wonder if he asked his undertaker for a refund.

263 I once went steady with an undertaker's son until I found out he wanted me just for my body.

☞Joan Rivers

264 The undertaker in our town was so slick that half the time he'd sell the widow a burial suit that came with two pair of pants.

265 With the cost of funerals today, going down is going up.

☞Milton Berle

266 My aunt had a very inexpensive funeral for my uncle. She couldn't afford a casket so she bought him a suit with six handles.

267 My grandfather was a very insignificant man. At his funeral the hearse followed the other cars.

☞Woody Allen

268 Everything is drive-through. They even have a burial service called Jump-in-the-Box.

☞Wil Shriner

269 At the graveside, the preacher reminded us that we came from dust and will return to dust. My son tugged my sleeve and said, "Upstairs, under my bed, someone is either coming or going."

270 I refused to attend his funeral. But I wrote a very nice letter explaining that I approved of it.

☞Mark Twain

271 The preacher asked if anyone would want to come forward and say some kind words about the deceased. We settled for a moment of silence.

272 My Aunt Gladiola refused to believe that Uncle Filbert was gone. She said, "Oh, he says he's dead, but you know how that man lied to me all his life."

---

273 Undertakers try to make you look as lifelike as possible, which defeats the whole purpose. It's hard to feel bad for somebody who looks better than you do.

☞Anita Wise

---

274 Uncle Festron asked that he be buried at sea. He said, "Just once I'd like to go for a boat ride without getting seasick."

---

275 Everybody cried at Uncle Motley's funeral. We had no idea he owed that much money around town.

---

276 Uncle Glingo requested that Aunt Festoonia sing "Amazing Grace" at his funeral. He always claimed that her singing could wake up the dead, and he figured it was worth a try.

---

277 Uncle Claven's will was contested. It wasn't the money; it was the part about "being of sound mind" that bothered everybody.

GOD'S BEAUTY

278 All God's creatures are beautiful, with the possible exception of the slug.

---

279 Mudpacks aren't good for the complexion. Did you ever see a pretty pig?

☞Jack E. Leonard

---

280 I'd like to come back as an oyster. Then I'd only have to be good from September until April.

☞Gracie Allen

---

281 Only God can make a tree, but I'm the guy who has to rake the leaves all fall.

---

282 A young ministerial student from the Smokey Mountains was assigned to his first church, which was located in the middle of Kansas. After settling in, he called home.

"Well, what's it like out there?" asked his mother.

"The church is small, but nice, the people are friendly..." his voice trailed off.

"Anything else?" his mother encouraged.

"The scenery could be better, I think the state tree of Kansas should be the telephone pole."

---

283 The same God who made the rivers to flow and the wind to blow, the birds to fly and the fish to swim, also made my Uncle Delsey who just sits there.

---

284 I just bought an ant farm. I don't know where I'm gonna find a tractor that small.

☞Steven Wright

---

285 God not only made the world a beautiful place, but He also brought it in under budget.

---

286 A scientist showing slides of the Grand Canyon explained, "It took two hundred million years to make this."

A man in the audience asked, "Was it a government project?"

☞Milton Berle

287 Any hotel room today in America is about a hundred dollars, but if you can see the ocean from your room, it's another hundred dollars. Now, you can swim in the ocean for free, but if you can see it from the room...

☞Jackie Mason

288 God not only made things beautiful, but also vast. The vast oceans, the vast skies, the vast mountains, and my Aunt Heldy.

289 Sponges grow in the ocean. I wonder how much deeper the ocean would be if that didn't happen.

☞Steven Wright

290 Sunsets are beautiful, but they always come late in the day when the lighting's not so good.

291 My Uncle Brilbo drinks a little too much. He sees beautiful sunsets every time he blinks.

292 Those sunsets in Hawaii. When you're there, the tension just oozes out of you. I don't care about anything. Like yesterday, Jimmy cracked corn ... and I don't care.

☞Howie Mandell

293 God made the roaring oceans, the majestic mountains, the rolling hills and valleys — and Kansas.

294 I just traveled to China by ship. Boy, there ought to be a law against making an ocean that wide.

☞Will Rogers

295 Beauty is only skin deep. Anything deeper than that is a rash.

296 Beauty is only skin deep. But who wants to look any deeper?

297 They say that beauty is only skin deep. Leave it to me to be born inside out.

☞Phyllis Diller

298 Our preacher told us "All things are beautiful in God's eyes," which was enough to get me to go off my diet.

GOD

299 Forgive, O Lord,
My little joke on Thee
And I'll forgive
Thy great big one on me.

☞Robert Frost

300 God knows all things and even He only gets half of the questions on Jeopardy.

301 It must be nice to know all things, but it would make it hard to get people interested in a game of Trivial Pursuit.

302 God knows all things, past, present, and future. Which means He must win the football pool in Heaven every week.

303 God can see into the future, which must take a lot of the fun out of reading a mystery novel.

304 God created man, but I could do better.

☞Erma Bombeck

305 I'm not denying that women are foolish. God Almighty made 'em to match the men.

☞George Eliot

306 When people look at me they have only one thought — There but for the grace of God...

☞Rodney Dangerfield

307 God always was and always will be. In that respect, He has a lot in common with taxes.

308 God had no beginning and will have no end. That reminds me of some of the soap operas on daytime television.

309 The teacher asked the Sunday school students, "If God is immortal and man is immortal, what is the difference?" One student said, "God's been doing it longer."

310 The Sunday school teacher asked why God is always pictured as an older being with white hair and beard. One student said, "They don't sell Grecian Formula in Heaven."

311 Gray hair is God's graffiti.

☞Bill Cosby

312 A father asked his young daughter what she was drawing. She said, "A picture of God." The father said, "Honey, no one knows what God looks like." She showed him her drawing and said, "They do now."

---

313 If God came down to me today and said, "Jack..." you know, He knows practically everybody.

☞Jack Benny

---

314 God is love, but get it in writing.

☞Mae West

---

315 My son claims that God is left handed. When I asked him why, he said, "He has to be. Every time I read about some holy person it says they're sitting on the right hand of God."

GRACE BEFORE MEALS

316 We always say Grace before meals at our house. It's a tradition. When my dad cooks, it's also a safety precaution.

---

317 We have a lot of hungry kids at our house. We say Grace before meals, but whoever says the slowest "amen" doesn't get as much to eat.

---

318 My Aunt Philby is not only a bad cook, but a dangerous one. At her house, Grace before meals lasts for 45 minutes.

---

319 At our house, we used to thank the Lord for our food, but when everybody else said "amen," I said, "Except for the broccoli."

...You see, I never considered broccoli a food. I considered it little green pieces of Hell on earth.

---

320 My Aunt Fanny was always very heavy, until she finally came up with a diet that worked. She began saying Grace *during* meals.

---

321 My brother, Frank, had the biggest appetite in the world. After Grace before meals he'd say "A" with his mouth empty, and "men" with his mouth full.

Frank was quick. We'd all bow our heads for Grace before meals. By the time we lifted them again, he was going for seconds.

---

322 Modern times are something else. When today's kids say "Give us this day our daily bread," they pause. They're waiting for the Good Lord to ask, "Would you like that in a plastic bag or paper?"

---

323 I don't think there was one time when I thanked the Lord for our food, that I didn't also thank my mom for making it so scrumptious.

---

324 When my sister cooked we said Grace before meals, and "Where's the Pepto-Bismol?" after meals.

---

325 We always bowed our heads before meals when my sister cooked. Partially to thank the Lord for the food He gave us, and partially out of embarrassment for what my sister had done to it.

---

326 We once thanked the Lord for a meal my sister had cooked and a voice from above said, "Don't blame Me for this meal. That food was all right when it was raw."

327 My sister is a very religious cook. Practically any meal she makes could turn out to be the last supper.

328 We say Grace differently when my sister cooks. We say, "Dear Lord, *protect* us from this food."

...Either that or we say, "Dear Lord, we thank You for what used to be food."

329 Once my sister got mad at the prayer we said and she shouted, "I'll get even with you for this." We looked at the food she had cooked and said, "We thought you had."

330 My brother never ate when Sis cooked. He was the designated driver ... to take the rest of us to the hospital.

331 A man sees a lion in the jungle. The man falls to his knees and starts praying. Lo and behold, the lion goes down on his knees next to him and also starts to pray. The man says, "It's a miracle." The lion says, "Please don't talk while I'm saying Grace!"

☞Milton Berle

THE GREAT FLOOD

332 The day before Noah left in the ark, the local TV weatherman predicted that it would be cloudy.

☞Milton Berle

---

333 During the Great Flood the entire world was under water. It gave a whole new meaning to the term "treading water."

...It was a great time to be amphibious.

---

334 If the Great Flood hit today, Miss Piggy wouldn't survive, but Kermit the Frog would.

---

335 During the Great Flood, sharks were heard to say to one another, "I don't know about you, but I'm stuffed."

336 While the water was rising, rattlesnakes could be heard saying to one another, "I should have listened to my mother. She always wanted me to be a water moccasin."

337 The only ones to survive were Noah, his family, the animals on the ark, and anyone who could hold his breath for 40 days and 40 nights.

338 During the Great Flood, the biggest understatement of the era was "Surf's up."

The dumbest statement of the era was "The farmers needed this."

339 Seasickness would have been the biggest epidemic of the time — if there had been anybody around to get it.

340 The Great Flood certainly drove down real estate prices — especially for homes with a pool.

HEAVEN

341 Yes, there is life after death. But please don't tell the IRS.

☞Mark Twain

342 My mom says that Heaven would be any place that doesn't have to be dusted every other day.

343 Heaven is a place where everyone is happy and content. So we must assume there are no taxes there.

344 Heaven for climate, Hell for society.

☞Mark Twain

345 My Uncle Fillpot knows that you can't take it with you so he's preparing to make some money after he gets to Heaven. He's studying to be a harp repairman.

346 If everybody in Heaven is happy, where do they send mothers-in-law?

347 A man died and went to Heaven and asked St. Peter, "Can I have a cigarette up here?"

St. Peter said, "Sure."

The man said, "Where can I get a light?"

St. Peter said, "For that, you have to go to Hell."

348 Heaven is a place where everybody is happy — except for those who can't stand harp music.

349 I felt sorry for one poor soul who didn't think he wanted to go to Heaven because he was afraid of heights.

...His preacher convinced him to lead a good life anyway and be buried with a parachute.

350 There is no illness in Heaven, which makes it tough on a hypochondriac who has led a good life.

...I imagine a hypochondriac at the Pearly Gates might say to St. Peter, "I'll go in, but could you do me a favor? Slam one of the gates on my foot."

---

351 There will be music in Heaven, so let's hope they have a soundproof section for teenagers.

...Heaven, to me, is when my kids finally turn off the music.

---

352 A woman got to the Pearly Gates, but St. Peter wouldn't let her in. Her name wasn't on the list. He said, "You'll have to go down below."

She begged, "Could I just say goodbye to my husband? He died long before I did. He told me if I was ever unfaithful to him, he would turn over in his grave."

St. Peter called to one of his assistants, "Go tell Whirling Willie his wife is here."

---

353 A minister met with a group of elderly ladies. He said, "Ladies, at your age, you should be thinking about the hereafter." One woman said, "Oh, I'm always thinking about the hereafter. Everytime I go to the refrigerator I think, what am I here after?"

354 I do not believe in an afterlife, although I am bringing a change of underwear.

☞Woody Allen

HELL

355 Maybe someday they'll come up with a microwave Hell. You can spend an eternity there in … maybe three and a half years.

356 My Uncle Philo is so dumb he'd try to open up a tanning salon in Hell.

357 I just came back from a terrible vacation and it dawns on me that the one good thing about being sent to Hell is that it's inexpensive.

358 Our preacher says that Hell is filled with brimstone, so if you're going there wear sensible shoes.

359 I don't know exactly where Hell is or what it's like, but if it's like every other place I've been to, it does have a gift shop.

---

360 Hell is where bad people go when they die. There's a little bar on the other side of town where they go when they're alive.

---

361 Hell is a place of fire and brimstone. It sounds like a great location for a lemonade stand.

---

362 Hell is like being kept after school forever.

---

363 Hell is like having a television set that only shows commercials.

---

364 Hell doesn't allow any visiting days, which is all right with me. A lot of my friends will be there anyway.

---

365 One man got to Heaven and there were only two people there — the Lord and George Washington. The man said, "Where are all the people?" The Lord said, "They're down below. Here, I'll show you."

The Lord opened up a hole in the clouds and the man could see down below. There was a big band and people were singing and dancing. The man asked, "How come people are singing and dancing, there's a big band playing down there, and nothing's going on up here?"

The Lord replied, "You don't think I'm gonna book a big band for two people, do you?"

HONESTY

366 Abraham Lincoln once walked over 10 miles in the snow just to pay a one penny fine on an overdue library book. I did the same thing once, but it had nothing to do with honesty. I had a crush on the librarian.

367 Always maintain your reputation for honesty — even if you have to lie to do it.

368 If you tell the truth, you don't have to remember anything.

☞Mark Twain

369 My mom always told me to tell the truth and shame the devil. Unfortunately, when I told the truth, the devil got off scot free and I was the one who was punished.

370 Honesty is the best policy, but insanity is a better defense.

☞Steve Landesberg

371 Honesty is always the best policy — even if it does cost you a fortune in taxes.

372 Honesty is the best policy, but it is not the cheapest.

☞Mark Twain

373 A thing worth having is a thing worth cheating for.

☞W. C. Fields

374 Anyone who starts out by saying, "I'll be honest with you," isn't.

375 Everytime Pinocchio told a lie his nose grew longer. Honesty was his only policy — until he discovered plastic surgery.

376 I was thrown out of college for cheating on my metaphysics final. I was looking into the soul of the boy sitting next to me.

☞Woody Allen

377 The one problem with being honest in business dealings is that it throws the whole system out of whack.

378 I knew one man who not only claimed to be honest, but even had his parole officer vouch for him.

379 I've got a brother-in-law. I don't say he's a thief — he just finds things before people lose them.

☞Henny Youngman

380 One gent I knew had an "Honest Business Person of the Year" award prominently displayed on his office wall. The plaque was stolen.

381 A kleptomaniac is a person who helps himself because he can't help himself.

☞Henry Morgan

382 One gentleman came home early from the country club. His wife said, "What happened? I thought you were playing golf today with Harry."

The gentleman said, "Would you play golf with someone who cheats on the course, lies about his score, and welshes on his bets?"

She said, "Of course not."

The guy said, "Well, neither would Harry."

383 A lie can travel halfway around the world while the truth is putting on its shoes.

☞Mark Twain

384 Never tell a lie — except for practice.

☞Mark Twain

385 I know many liars doing very well these days — making out airline schedules.

☞Shelley Berman

386 A preacher was playing in a game of high stakes poker with three other gentlemen when the police raided it. Quickly they all hid the evidence from the authorities.

The police asked the first man, "Were you gambling?"

The man said, "I must not tell a lie. I was not gambling."

The police asked the second man, "Were you gambling?" He said, "I can't tell a lie. No, I was not gambling."

They asked the third man if he was gambling. He said, "I'm telling you the honest truth — I was not gambling."

The police asked the preacher, "Reverend, were you gambling?

The preacher said, "With whom?"

387 Thou shalt not steal — only from other comedians.

☞W. C. Fields

388 Always maintain an honest reputation. It makes it that much easier to get away with a lie when you really need one.

389 Some people believe honesty is the best policy if they can't get away with anything else.

390 Always tell the truth. Remember, there are other games to play besides golf.

391 I thought I had won the "Liar's Competition," but it turns out the judges weren't telling the truth.

392 One politician claimed, "I am as honest as the day is long."
His friend said, "Here's $100 bucks."

The politician replied, "Wasn't that a lovely sunset?"

HONOR THY FATHER AND MOTHER

393 Most vegetables are something God invented to let mothers get even with their children.

☞P. J. O'Rourke

---

394 When I was a small child, I always obeyed my parents. It was a small price to pay for free room and board.

---

395 I always did exactly what my parents told me to do. It was easier than making decisions for myself.

---

396 My mom wanted me to become a doctor. My dad said, "Just become something you're good at." So I became good at not being a doctor.

---

397 My mom always demanded OOE — Obedience Or Else.

398 I idolized my mother. I didn't realize she was a lousy cook until I went into the Army.

☞Jackie Gayle

399 I know how to do anything — I'm a Mom.

☞Roseanne

400 My father taught me early on to respect authority. For a long time I thought "authority" was anyone with a removable belt.

401 Adam had a lot of trouble buying his father a Father's Day gift. What can you buy somebody who has everything?

☞Milton Berle

402 If we children misbehaved, Mom would send us to bed without our supper. For me it was a deterrent; for my brother it was a diet plan.

403 One day Mom yelled at me, "Someday you'll have children of your own." I said, "Mom, who else's children would I have?"

404 The proudest day of my life was when I could say to my parents, "You've always worked hard to provide things for me. Now it's time to go out and work hard for yourself."

405 My brother was worse. He said, "Mom, you've been bending over a hot stove all your life. Straighten up."

406 I knew one gentleman who wrote a nice, sincere letter to his parents thanking them for their help and support in putting him through law school. A week later they got the bill for "preparing one Thank You letter."

407 I'm very loyal in relationships. Even when I go out with my mom I don't look at other moms.

☞ Garry Shandling

408 I always honored my father and mother. After all, they controlled the allowance strings.

409 My mother finally admitted in her later years that the easiest way for her to get me to do something was to forbid me to do it.

410 When I asked my mother "why?" She'd always say, "Because I said so, that's why." It was excellent training for filing my tax returns.

411 My mother was very honest. She said, "You should obey me because you love me, and also because if you don't, I'll tell your father."

412 My buddy's mother once told him, "You just wait until your father gets home." They've been waiting for 32 years now.

HUMILITY

413 Humility is a funny virtue. Once you think you've got it, you've lost it.

---

414 What the world needs is more geniuses with humility. There are so few of us left.

☞Oscar Levant

---

415 I never travel without my diary. One should always have something sensational to read.

☞Oscar Wilde

---

416 Humility is one of those virtues that's not so much for you as for those around you.

---

417 I like being around humble people. It makes it that much easier for me to show off.

---

418 I would like to be humble, but why lie?

419 One gentleman said, "I've taken a good look at myself and I have every virtue but humility. What can I do to acquire it?" I said, "Look again."

420 One gentleman asked me, "Is it possible to be too humble?" I said, "Not with your record."

421 For some people humility is a virtue; for others it's just a statement of fact.

422 My wife says her job is to keep me humble, whatever that is.

☞Bob Hope

423 I like being around truly humble people. Less to listen to.

424 I'm very humble. I used to be boastful, but people kept tripping me up.

425 I've personally found that it's much easier to be humble when you have good reason to be.

426 I don't like to brag, but with my natural abilities, humility comes easy to me.

427 I enjoy being humble. It's good for my ego.

428 It's not good to be too humble — people might start believing you.

429 Truly great people are usually truly humble. I wouldn't know since I have very little experience with either.

430 I can never tell whether I'm being humble or merely honest.

IF GOD HAD MEANT FOR ...

431 If God had meant for us to fly, we all would have been born with a bottom that could be used as a floatation device.

432 If the Good Lord had wanted us to fly, He would have made it simpler for people to get to the airport.

☞Milton Berle

433 If God had meant for us to travel so much on business, we would have been born with luggage tags instead of ears.

434 If God had meant for us to eat peanut butter, he would have given us teflon gums.

☞Bob Orben

435 If God had meant for us to work seven days a week, He wouldn't have invented professional football.

436 If God had meant for woman to cook all the time, we would have been born with frying pans where our hands are.

437 I don't work out. If God had intended for me to bend over, He would have put diamonds on the floor.

☞Joan Rivers

438 If God had meant for me to be a vegetarian, He would have made spinach taste like chicken fried steak.

439 If God had meant for me to be smart, I would have been born with all the answers ... instead I was born not even knowing a lot of the questions.

440 It became apparent to me that if God wanted me to play tennis, He would have given me less leg and more room to store the ball.

☞Erma Bombeck

441 If God had meant for us to watch television all day, He would have arranged for some better programs.

442 If God had meant for man to be happy all the time, He would have made golf an easier game.

443 If God had meant for all of us to get along peacefully at all times, He would have had no need to create lawyers.

444 If God had made it easy for all of us to get to Heaven, we'd have to live with the riff-raff up there, too.

JUDGMENT DAY

445 I wonder if on judgment day we'll be allowed to have a lawyer present?

446 I've led a very dull life. I hope on judgment day I don't doze off.

447 Judgment day should be interesting. It should be like playing "Jeopardy" except for really great prizes.

448 You can't lie on judgment day. Well, you could but it would just make matters worse.

449 You know who I'll really feel sorry for? The guy on judgment day who hollers, "Let's make it the best two out of three."

450 On judgment day everybody will see everything we've done all our lives. I plan to get there early and get a seat way in the back.

451 When your life flashes before you, do you think that includes every trip you made to the bank?

☞Carol Leifer

452 I think I know what I'll say to God on judgment day — "Can I take a make-up test?"

453 The trouble with money is — you may not have time to count it on judgment day.

☞Milton Berle

454 A real snob is a person who shows up at the last judgment and complains about the seating arrangement.

455 When my Uncle Delphine heard that everybody who ever lived would be present at the last judgment, his first question was "I wonder if they'll have an open bar?"

456 Our preacher told me all my sins would be shown to everybody on judgment day. He said, "What will you do then?" I said, "Try to pretend I'm somebody else."

457 Everyone who ever lived will be present for judgment day. Boy, wouldn't you love to have the name tag concession for that meeting?

458 We're going to see the life of everyone who ever lived at the last judgment ... so pack a lunch.

...You know they've got to run out of popcorn.

459 You'll be held accountable for all your misdeeds on the day of the last judgment. It's like a tax audit...for keeps.

The only good part is you don't have to bring receipts.

...Or pay an accountant.

460 We should all lead the kind of life where we can show up on judgment day and say, "OK, where do I pick up my prizes?"

KNEELING

461 Some people get up on their high horse when they should be getting down on their knees.

462 The only time I pray is when I lose a contact lens. I hate to get down on my knees for only one reason.

...Besides, those things are hard to find.

463 I pray for courage. I get down on my knees to ask God to help me stand on my own two feet.

464 After a certain age, we get down on our knees to say a prayer that we'll be able to get back up again.

465 My Uncle Knively begins every morning on his knees. His dog keeps hiding his overalls under the porch.

466 My Uncle Delford only gets down on one knee to pray. He claims he only gets half the things he prays for anyway.

467 My Aunt Grindola is so heavy that we never know when she's praying. Her body looks the same when she's kneeling as when she's standing.

468 Our football team kneels down and says a prayer before every game. We haven't won a game yet. Unfortunately, the other team prays, too … and they're usually better than we are.

469 My Uncle Wormly says he gets down on his knees for three reasons — to ask for something, to give thanks for something, and when he doesn't have change for the pay toilets at the bus stop.

LIFE

470 Now that I've learned to make the most of life, most of it is gone.

☞Henny Youngman

471 Life is something for us to do from here to eternity.

472 Life is a series of inspired follies. The difficulty is to find them to do.

☞George Bernard Shaw

473 Life consists not in holding good cards, but playing well those you hold.

☞Josh Billings

474 Life is much too important a thing to ever talk seriously about it.

☞Oscar Wilde

475 Life is what happens to you while you're busy making other plans.

☞John Lennon

476 Existence is a wonderful gift. It's the only thing that comes with a real lifetime guarantee.

477 My mom used to say, "I'm dying to know the mystery of life."

478 How can we say life is short when it ends with eternity?

479 Showing up is 80% of life.

☞Woody Allen

480 From time to time we ask ourselves, "Why was I born?" It's when others start asking that about us that we're in trouble.

481 Life is the waiting room to eternity. It's the only waiting room where no one ever says, "Hey, I should have gone ahead of him."

482 I Finally figured out the only reason to be alive is to enjoy it.

☞Rita Mae Brown

483 Life is short — except for those years when your children are teenagers.

484 What is human life? The first third a good time; the rest remembering it.

☞Mark Twain

485 You only go around once in life — unless you're the kind of person who has bad luck with tornadoes.

486 Cats, they say, have nine lives, but I'll bet when they get to the seventh or eighth life their insurance premiums skyrocket.

487 You have to go through life before you can get to Heaven. It's a lot like eating your broccoli before you get any dessert.

488 Before we had life we were just a lump of clay. With some people today, it's hard to notice the transition.

489 Yesterday's the past, tomorrow's the future, but today is a GIFT. That's why it's called the present.

☞Bil Keane

LOAVES AND FISHES

490 The multiplication of the loaves and fishes was not only an impressive miracle, but also a handy idea for when unexpected company arrives.

491 Thousands were fed with five loaves and two fishes and they collected leftovers after the meal. They had to. They ran out of doggie bags.

492 Not only did they feed thousands with five loaves and two fishes, but afterwards, hundreds of people asked for the recipe.

493 Some food chains today can serve thousands of hamburgers with just one or two pounds of ground beef.

494 The most unappreciative person at the multiplication of the loaves and fishes was the fellow who after the meal turned to the person next to him and said, "You wouldn't happen to have any gum, would you?"

495 A multitude was served with five loaves and two fishes — and this was hundreds of years before airplane food was even invented.

496 All those loaves and fishes were free, too. Otherwise the twelve Apostles would have been known as the twelve Vendors.

497 Sometimes it's hard to satisfy people. Thousands were fed with five loaves and two fishes yet afterwards a few were heard to mutter, "What? No dessert?"

498 Thousands were fed with just five loaves and two fishes. It was an astounding miracle, if rather a limited menu.

It was a miracle that delighted everyone — with the possible exception of the Jordan River Catering Service.

499 I cast my bread upon the water tonight. Of course, my wife said it was soup.

☞Milton Berle

LOVE THY NEIGHBOR

500 Love is a feeling you feel when you're about to feel a feeling you never felt before.

☞Flip Wilson

---

501 I tried loving my enemies but it didn't work. After you love them long enough you start getting them mixed up with your friends.

---

502 The Bible says to love your enemy. So I sent my enemy a Bible. Let her learn to love me for awhile.

---

503 Love your enemies — just long enough for them to drop their guard.

---

504 My neighbor is built like a truck. The other day she was standing beside a parking meter and somebody stole her kneecaps.

☞Phyllis Diller

---

505 Love thy enemy. It irritates them like crazy.

506 The doctor opened the window wide. He said, "Now, stick your tongue out." I said, "What for?" He said, "I'm mad at my neighbors."

☞Milton Berle

507 Love thy neighbor — at least until he returns thy lawnmower.

508 My neighbor is a real showoff. He's got a lawnmower with bucket seats.

☞Milton Berle

509 I have a neighbor who has memorized 4000 telephone numbers. Unfortunately, she can't remember the names that go with them.

☞Ernie Kovacs

510 Love thy neighbor. If everyone followed that advice it would sure take a lot of the zing out of backyard gossip.

511 Love thy neighbor, but keep the fence in good repair, too.

512 The Bible tells us that we should love our neighbors. Did the Bible mention that they'd have a kid who plays the drums?

☞Milton Berle

513 Love your neighbor ... love your enemy. If everyone followed those principles it could be the end of partisan politics as we know it today.

514 My mother used to say that she loved everyone. I said, "Did you ever tell Aunt Bertha that you loved her?" She said, "How could I? I'm not talking to her."

I said, "The Bible says to love thy enemy." Mom said, "Aunt Bertha's not my enemy; she's my sister."

MIRACLES

515 I'm going to give my psychoanalyst one more year, then I'm going to Lourdes.

☞Woody Allen

516 I believe in miracles. In fact, it's a major part of my weight loss program.

517 I have to believe in miracles. My boss says it's the only way I'll ever get another raise.

518 I think television is a miracle — that anyone ever watches it.

519 Changing water into wine is a miracle. Nowadays, it's also a federal offense.

520 My preacher worked two miracles in church last Sunday. Two people were awake at the end of his sermon.

521 The IRS is a good example; they perform two miracles every year. Getting blood from a stone is one miracle. And getting the stone to fill out its own forms is another.

522 I believe in miracles. It's either that or give up golf altogether.

523 I'll tell you about a miracle. Last month they put the heart of a turtle into a human being. Last week the patient walked out of the hospital! Thursday he got to his car in the parking lot.

☞Norm Crosby

524 I played golf with Billy Graham. Every time it was my turn to putt, the hole healed up.

☞Bob Hope

525 There's an example of a miracle in my own family. My Uncle Belnon was struck head-on by lightning. He's not only alive to this day, but he makes an excellent night light.

526 Our Sunday school teacher told us, "A miracle is an event that transcends known physical laws and hence appears to be thaumaturgic in nature. Now can

115

anyone give me an example of a miracle?"

I raised my hand and said, "You thinking that any of us would know what 'transcends' and 'thaumaturgic' mean."

---

527 My friend Wally said, "I'll give you an example of a miracle. My Uncle Fesnick came home very late one night and told Aunt Matilda that he was walking along the road when he was blinded by the headlights of an oncoming vehicle. He couldn't move and was about to be struck when an angel swooped down and lifted him from the path of the speeding automobile.

"He said he was so grateful that he insisted that he be allowed to buy the angel a drink. Well, he did, he said, and that angel just drank and drank and that's why Uncle Fesnick came home in the condition he was in.

A week later he was almost hit by a bus and that same angel saved his life again and he had no choice but to treat him to another few drinks."

The teacher said, "Those aren't miracles; they're just tall tales."

Wally giggled, "I know that. But after hearing the first one, Aunt Matilda letting Uncle Fesnick live long enough to tell the second — that's the miracle."

MORALS

528 Always do what's right — if for no other reason than it's generally cheaper.

---

529 Always do right. This will gratify some people, and astonish the rest.

☞Mark Twain

---

530 Two wrongs never make a right, so why bother with the first wrong in the first place?

---

531 When you come to a fork in the road, always choose the path of righteousness. You'll hit far less traffic.

---

532 Immorality — the morality of those who are having a better time.

☞H. L. Mencken

533 Be careful. When the right thing is too easy, it may be the wrong thing.

534 Sometimes doing the right thing is actually easier than thinking up a good excuse for not doing it.

535 An ethical man is a Christian holding four aces.

☞Mark Twain

536 Live your life as if each day will be your last. One of these times you'll be right.

537 Why is it that every bad action has a good excuse?

538 When I'm good, I'm very good. And when I'm bad, I'm even better.

☞Mae West

539 Do unto others as you would have them do unto you. They probably won't, but do it anyway.

540 Try to do the right thing all day long. It's so tiring you'll sleep better at night.

541 The world was divided into good and bad people. The good ones slept better while the bad ones seemed to enjoy the waking hours much more.

☞Woody Allen

542 Try to lead your whole life as if your mother has just said, "Wait till your father gets home."

543 To be good is noble; but to show others how to be good is nobler and no trouble.

☞Mark Twain

544 Some people have trouble telling right from wrong. My Uncle Fenlow has trouble telling right from left.

... It costs him $2000 a year for collision insurance — just to go square dancing.

545 Good morals mean doing the right thing even when God blinks.

546 My mom had a simple definition of morality: "Always do the right thing because it's the right thing to do."

547 Fewer things are harder to put up with than a good example.

☞Mark Twain

548 Morality means living your life in such a way that when it comes time for the last judgment, you won't be afraid to volunteer to go first.

MORTALITY

549 Death is nature's way of saying, "Your table is ready."

☞Robin Williams

---

550 I have to learn to accept my own mortality. I much prefer accepting other people's.

---

551 If man were immortal, do you realize what his meat bills would be?

☞Woody Allen

---

552 It's a funny old world — a man's lucky if he can get out of it alive.

☞W. C. Fields

---

553 Death is a part of life — the very last part.

---

554 Death is the original "once-in-a-lifetime" experience.

555 Death comes to each of us just once. But so far it seems once has been enough.

556 Lazarus is the only person who died twice. It had something to do with the fine print in his insurance policy.

557 The only thing wrong with immortality is that it tends to go on forever.

☞Herb Caen

558 How come life is so short but we stay dead for so long?

559 We are all mortal, so if you buy anything that's guaranteed to last forever, you're being taken.

560 If Shaw and Einstein couldn't beat death, what chance have I got?

☞Mel Brooks

561 Look on the bright side — we all come into this world with a lifetime guarantee.

562 When I die I'm going to leave my body to science fiction.

☞Steven Wright

563 This guy dies and leaves the shortest will. It says, "Being of sound mind, I spent my money."

☞Henny Youngman

564 None of us are ever sure if we'll see tomorrow. In fact, sometimes I have trouble remembering yesterday.

565 It is impossible to experience one's own death objectively and still carry a tune.

☞Woody Allen

566 My preacher asked me, "What will you do if the Angel of Death rings your doorbell tomorrow?" I said, "Absolutely nothing. My doorbell hasn't worked in 15 years."

---

567 We're all mortal. Except that Aunt Belvie says that Uncle Drim will never die. He doesn't have enough ambition.

---

568 And Uncle Drim says he knows his life won't last forever, but being married to Aunt Belvie sure makes it seem that way.

---

569 It's hard to believe that my life will have an end. As far as some people are concerned, it hasn't really had a beginning yet.

---

570 My Grandmom always used to say, "Dying ain't so bad if the living has been good."

---

571 I'm not afraid of death. It's the make-over at the undertaker's that scares me.

☞Anita Wise

NOAH'S ARK

572 Noah took a male and female of each species on his ark for 40 days and 40 nights. It was the world's first honeymoon cruise.

---

573 I told my son that all the animals on Noah's ark came in pairs. He said, "Except for the worms. They came in apples."

---

574 When Noah's ark finally settled on dry land, Noah was so happy he said, "What can we do to celebrate?" His kids said, "Let's go to the zoo."

---

575 Even Noah got no salary for the first six months — partly on account of the weather and partly because he was learning navigation.

☞Mark Twain

---

576 After the water subsided all the animals had to get off the ark. The centipedes said, "Darn it, just when we were getting our sea legs."

577 The only reason my mother-in-law wasn't on Noah's ark was because they couldn't find another animal that looked like her.

☞Phyllis Diller

578 Noah's ark was a rough voyage for the animals. Even the hyenas had stopped laughing about it.

579 None of the animals had anything to wear on the ark. The elephants were the only ones who thought to bring their trunks.

580 If Noah had forgotten to put two herrings in the ark, half of Far Rockaway would have starved to death years ago.

☞Sam Levenson

581 It rained the whole time Noah was at sea, which wreaked havoc with the top deck shuffleboard tournament.

582 Noah had thousands of animals on his ark for 40 days and 40 nights. It preserved all of the species, but it ruined the resale value of the ark.

583 Noah must have taken into the ark two taxes, and did they multipy bountifully.

☞Will Rogers

584 After many days, a dove returned to the ark carrying an olive branch. All of the animals shouted, "But we sent you for pizza."

585 All of the animals had to pay their expenses before they could get off the ark except for the platypuses, who said: "Just put it on our bill."

586 When Noah had the two horseflies on his ark for 40 days, why didn't he swat them?

587 Noah had it tough. He took two of everything on the ark. First day at sea he lost one cuff link.

588 The animals who suffered the most on the ark were the zebras. Everything Noah did was in alphabetical order.

589 The cattle were unhappy on the ark. One turned to the other and said, "It's going to be tough trying to put together a decent stampede."

590 The two roaches were nervous during the entire trip. They kept wondering if Noah also brought along two exterminators.

591 The dumbest thing on the ark happened about the first week of the trip — Noah held a "Singles Only" party.

592 Everybody was very crowded on the ark — except, of course, for the porcupines.

593 Two of all the animals rode on the ark — except for the skunks, they were towed along behind in a dinghy.

594 Only two of each species were allowed on the ark. The kangaroos even had to empty their pockets before boarding.

595 Only two of everything were allowed. It was very tough on the three-toed sloths.

596 Finally the ark came to a standstill on Mount Ararat. The animals debarked. Two elephants walked off. Two lions. Two tigers. The four gnus came down the gangplank. A spectator was surprised to see four animals of one kind. Noah explained, "First there's the good gnus and then there's the bad gnus!" ☞Milton Berle

ORIGINAL SIN

597 The devil tempted Adam and Eve with an apple and they succumbed. We haven't gotten much better over the years, but at least we've gotten more sophisticated.

598 Adam and Eve committed the first sin. Some people will do anything to get into the Guinness Book of Records.

599 Adam and Eve committed the original sin together. It's a good thing, too. If one stayed in the Garden of Eden and the other one didn't, they wouldn't have had too many descendants, would they?

...I don't recall that the Garden of Eden had connubial visitation.

600 Adam and Eve committed the first sin. Big deal! They didn't have a heckuva lot of competition.

601 The day after that original sin, the sports page said, "Devil-1 — Adam and Eve-0."

..."They're both sent to the minors."

602 Adam and Eve were very content until that original sin and the birth of their first child. Then they started raising Cain.

603 Actually Cain wanted to commit the original sin but he wasn't Abel.

604 A sin takes on new and real terrors when there seems a chance that it is going to be found out.

☞Mark Twain

605 The wages of sin are death. But after taxes are taken out, it's just sort of a tired feeling.

☞Paula Poundstone

606 Did you know in my religion the sin of eating bread on Passover is comparable to the sin of adultery? I told this to a friend of mine and he told me he had tried them both and he couldn't see the comparison.

☞Jackie Mason

THE OTHER CHEEK

607 One of my classmates hit me, so I turned the other cheek. He hit me with his other hand.

---

608 I had to turn the other cheek. The doctor told me one shot of penicillin wouldn't be enough.

---

609 An eye for an eye and a tooth for a tooth. Boy, that's one swap meet I don't want to go to.

---

610 One day a kid in school hit me, so I asked my mother what I should do. She said, "Whatever the Bible says." So the next day I went back and "smote" him.

...I "smote" him pretty good, too. Blood began to issue from his nose.

611 First I turn one cheek, then I turn the other cheek. Then I turn nasty.

612 I've turned the other cheek so often, the first cheek has whiplash.

613 The airlines are making seats that are so narrow, turning the other cheek isn't a virtue, it's a necessity.

☞Robert Orben

614 You know you need to lose some weight when every time you turn the other cheek it takes five or six minutes for all the flesh to stop jiggling.

615 My mom taught me to turn the other cheek; my dad taught me how to fight. He said, "Develop a good left hook and let the other guy turn the other cheek for awhile."

616 Dad always said, "You can turn the other cheek if you want to, but you should let them know that if they hit one cheek too many, it may be the last cheek they ever hit."

---

617 My Uncle Gumley believed in turning the other cheek and it cost him his job. He was a boxer.

---

618 Uncle Gumley turned the other cheek so often he turned it into a broken jaw.

...He turned the other cheek one time and his opponent refused it. He said, "I'm not done hitting this one yet."

---

619 Uncle Gumley not only turned both cheeks, but threw in his nose occasionally as a bonus.

...His nose was flattened so much he had to learn to breath through his ears.

PESTILENCE AND PLAGUE

620 They had many plagues in the Old Testament. Nowadays we have only one — it's called taxes.

621 Many times in the Old Testament they were overrun with locusts. Now we seem to be overrun with politicians.

...At least when you step on a locust he doesn't come up for reelection.

622 For Daylight Savings Time in the Old Testament, they'd set their plagues back an hour.

623 They had a lot of tribulation in the Old Testament. It must have cost a fortune for plague insurance back then.

624 Every time Moses turned around there was another plague. Finally, somebody wised up and said, "Hey Moses, quit turning around."

625 In the Old Testament they had plagues and pestilence. In fact, one of the biggest plagues was learning how to spell "pestilence."

626 They had four seasons in the Old Testament: Plague, Summer, Pestilence and Winter.

627 I couldn't put up with all the plagues and pestilence. If I had lived back then, I would have moved to another Testament.

628 They were periodically overrun with frogs, locust, lizards, snakes — it was tough to be an animal activist back then.

629 That's one of the few things we know about the people of the Old Testament — they were plague prone.

PILLAR OF SALT

630 One of the biggest jokes in the Old Testament was when someone would say to Lot, "Hey Lot, how's your wife?"
   He'd say, "Needs more salt."

631 It's a strange punishment to turn someone into a pillar of salt. Maybe God felt she was like a minor league ballplayer — needed more seasoning.

632 Lot was very upset when they were at sea and his wife was suddenly turned into a pillar of salt. It meant he now had to do all the rowing.

633 As Lot was getting his wife out of the boat he dropped her. He immediately picked her up and threw her over his left shoulder for luck.

634 What do you do if you have a wife who is turned into a pillar of salt? Sit her on the table next to the pillar of pepper?

One thing you should never do is leave her out in the rain.

...unless she's trying to lose some weight.

635 If it happened today, Lot would make a fortune writing a book about it — "My Wife the Condiment."

636 Imagine having to kiss your wife goodbye after she's been turned into a pillar of salt. I'll bet that'd leave a bitter taste in your mouth.

637 What happened to Lot's wife was an inconvenience for Lot, too. Neighbors were constantly knocking on his door and asking to borrow a cup of salt.
...They knew he had plenty.

638 It must be tough having a pillar of salt for a spouse — especially if you're supposed to be on a low sodium diet.

639 When Lot turned and saw his wife he immediately said to himself, "Hey, I bet she'd be good sprinkled on pretzels."

640 Lot said to his wife, "What happened?" She said, "I don't know. All of a sudden I've got this terrible thirst … and deer keep trying to lick the back of my head."

---

641 That's the last time I play golf with Billy Graham. I sank one putt and he turned my caddy into a pillar of salt.

☞Bob Hope

PRAYER

642 I was in the supermarket the other day. I thought I was in church. Women were walking up the aisles saying, "Oh my God."

☞Henny Youngman

---

643 Congress opens every session with a prayer. It's good to see politicians pray. It keeps their hands up where we can see them.

---

644 My mom taught me early on that God answers all my prayers — but sometimes the answer is "no."

645 Even if only a few of my prayers are answered it's still cheaper than golf lessons.

646 One man went to church and prayed for a raise. His boss fired him for going over his head.

☞Milton Berle

647 Did you hear about the scientist who crossed a praying mantis with a termite, and now he has a bug that says Grace before it eats your house.

☞Henny Youngman

648 The new technology is getting into everything. I said a prayer yesterday and got God's answering machine.

649 It was a sad day when the Supreme Court ruled that we could not have prayer in school. It meant the kids had to study for their exams.

650 I always prayed when I went to school, but the teacher never did turn into a pillar of salt.

651 They can't eliminate prayer in the schools. How else could students pass a true-false test?

☞Milton Berle

652 I've always been an advocate of prayer in school. It was the only way I could get a date for the senior prom.

653 The teachers all want prayer in school. It's the only chance they've got of ever getting a decent raise.

654 No matter what the Supreme Court says, you can still bow your head and say a silent prayer in school. Just tell the teacher you're checking to see if your fly is open.

655 The teacher said, "Hey, what are you kids in the back of the class doing on your knees?" One kid said, "We're shooting craps." The teacher said, "Oh, that's OK. I thought you were praying."

---

656 My daughter was leading her son in his nightly prayers. After he had said all his "God blesses," she reminded him "Ask God to make you a good boy." My grandson said, "Oh, I don't have to be a good boy tomorrow. We're going to Grandmom's, remember?"

---

657 A preacher kept praying every night to hit the lottery. He'd say, "Dear Lord, I'm not asking for me, but our church is poor, we need money to do Your work. Please let us hit the lottery." He didn't win.

He prayed and he prayed and he prayed until he almost dispaired.

Finally, one night the Lord appeared to him. The preacher said, "I shouldn't even talk to You. I've prayed to hit the lottery, but nothing happens. Why?"

The Lord said, "Do me one favor, will you? Buy a ticket."

658 One gentleman led a good life. So when he prayed that he would hit the lottery, his prayers were answered. He immediately went out and bought new clothes. He got himself a facelift, a tummy tuck, brand new teeth, and a very expensive toupee.

He was driving along in his sporty new Ferrari when a truck smashed into him. He went one way, the teeth went another, the toupee went in a third direction.

When he got to Heaven he said to the Lord, "Everything was going so good, why did You let that happen to me?"

The Lord said, "To tell you the truth, Sam, I didn't know it was you."

659 The plane was going up and down and sideways. A little old lady got nervous. She shouted, "Everyone on the plane pray." I said, "I don't know how to pray." She said, "Well, do something religious." So I started a bingo game.

☞Henny Youngman

660 Now I lay me down to sleep
I pray the Lord my soul to keep.
If I should die before I wake,
The dog can have my leftover
steak.

REINCARNATION

661 Do you believe in reincarnation?I
eat it every day. It's called hash.

☞Milton Berle

662 The one good thing about
reincarnation is you don't have to bring
much luggage.

663 I prefer not to believe in
reincarnation. I've lived one good life,
and that's plenty.

664 There has never been an
intelligent person of the age of sixty who
would consent to live his life over again.
His or anyone else's.

☞Mark Twain

665 Everybody who believes in reincarnation says they were a King or a Queen in their past lives. Nobody was ever a bag lady.

666 If I had my life to live over again, I wouldn't have the time.

☞Bob Hope

667 If I had my life to live over again, I wouldn't have the strength to do it.

☞Joe E. Lewis

668 If you had to live your life over again, don't do it.

☞Henny Youngman

669 Some people claim they were Napoleon in a past life. My Uncle Thelby thinks he's Napoleon in this life.

670 If there were such a thing as reincarnation our birth certificates would be issued as a return ticket.

671 My Uncle Pylar hopes there's reincarnation because he's so cheap. He says if he can't take it with him, he's coming back to get it.

672 It would be nice if our Founding Fathers would come back — and tell us what they really meant when they wrote the Constitution.

673 If there were such a thing as reincarnation then Heaven would only be a place where you stop off to pick up clean laundry.

674 You show me a person who believes in reincarnation and I'll show you a person who's just begging for a chance to come back and do it right.

675 There has to be something to reincarnation. I couldn't have gotten this far behind in just one lifetime.

☞Milton Berle

676 Some undertakers approve of reincarnation. It's a chance for repeat business.

677 It's not easy to lead a good life. Why would we want to lead 10 or 12?

678 If there were such a thing as reincarnation, tombstones wouldn't be carved in marble — they'd be written lightly in pencil.

679 Just in case there is reincarnation, I'm making out my will so that I leave all my money to whoever I'm going to be next.

680 If there were such a thing as reincarnation, we'd all be born with a yo-yo string instead of an umbilical cord.

681 If Marie Antoinette comes back, she's got to be eight to ten inches shorter.

RELIGIOUS ARTICLES

682 It's hard for religious Catholics to get fire insurance. Too many candles in the house!

☞Milton Berle

---

683 We had so many religious articles around our house, it looked like a Hall of Fame for holy people.

---

684 We had so many religious articles around the house, I was eight years old before I found out I didn't live in Heaven.

---

685 My mom loved to buy religious articles. She was a statue-aholic.

---

686 Our house was broken into four times, but nothing was ever taken. We wound up with four converts instead.

---

687 Yes sir, if you were in the New Testament, my mom had a picture of you somewhere around the house.

688 Mom had nothing but religious pictures in our house. The only way I could get her to display my graduation picture was to have the photographer add a halo to it.

689 I had a picture of the Beatles in my room, but I had to tell Mom it was Matthew, Mark, Luke, and John.

Convincing her that they played guitars was the hard part.

But I never could hang up that picture of Willie Nelson. Mom said he looked too much like Judas Iscariot.

690 Everything in our house had religious overtones. Even the toy boat I used to play with in the bathtub was a replica of Noah's ark.

691 My mother was such a bad driver that when she pulled onto a freeway the St. Christopher statue would crawl into the glove compartment.

SERMONS

692 I have no idea what color my preacher's eyes are. When he prays he closes his; when he preaches he closes mine.

---

693 He was a terrific preacher. At the end of his sermon there was a great awakening.

☞Milton Berle

---

694 The sermon had been going on endlessly. Finally the minister's voice cracked and said, "What more can I say?" One parishioner yelled, "How about 'Amen!' "

☞Milton Berle

---

695 The preacher asked his congregation, "About what should I preach?"

Someone answered, "About 15 minutes."

---

696 The first time I took my daughter to Sunday services, I asked what she thought of it. She said, "The commercial was too long."

---

697 Few sinners are saved after the first twenty minutes of a sermon.

☞Mark Twain

---

698 Our preacher gives fiery sermons. That means it's like Hell sitting through them ... and they seem to last an eternity.

---

699 Our preacher likes to talk so much that a committee had to go and tell him. They said, "Reverend, we call them Sunday services because they're supposed to begin and end on the same day."

---

700 Our preacher likes to hear himself talk. After the first 35 minutes, he's about the only one who does.

---

701 He was a preacher and never charged nothing for his preaching ... and it was worth it, too.

☞Mark Twain

702 Our preacher uses humor extensively. About three or four times during his sermons, I find myself waking up laughing.

703 When the Good Lord told His Apostles to go and preach the Gospel, He should have set a time limit on each sermon.

704 Our pastor preaches fire and brimstone, but after about 25 minutes we'd like to dip him in tar and feathers.

705 Our preacher told us his sermons should educate and motivate. One parishioner added, "After a certain amount of time, they should also terminate."

706 Our preacher began his sermon by saying, "I'm going to give a short discourse on the evils of lying." He lied.

SEVEN DEADLY SINS

707 I asked Uncle Willie to name the Seven Deadly Sins. He said, "Pride, Envy, Sloth, Greed ... Sneezy, Sleepy, and Dopey."

708 My Uncle Climbo says there's only one Deadly Sin. He got up to sloth and didn't have the energy for the rest of them.

709 I married for richer, for poorer, for better, for worse. Fang has been too lazy to be any of those things.

☞Phyllis Diller

710 Scientists announced today that they have discovered a cure for apathy. However, no one has shown much interest in it.

☞George Carlin

711 My Uncle Slide wonders how come we have Ten Commandments but only Seven Deadly Sins. He says, "It seems like we're getting the short end of the stick."

My Uncle Lumbo says, "Not really." He says, "As far as I'm concerned, lust counts as three.

---

712 Pride is a sin, except for some of us who are so doggone good at what we're doing that we can't avoid it.

---

713 They say that pride goeth before a fall. Then my Uncle Ferdel must have it. He keeps falling down every Friday night on his way home.

---

714 My Uncle Slink really is greedy. There are only Seven Deadly Sins and he has eight of them.

---

715 If you had everything, where would you put it?

☞Steven Wright

---

716 Uncle Slink really believes in greed. He says, "Money can't buy happiness, but it sure can make your gloom a lot more comfortable."

---

717 There are more important things in the world than money, but they won't go out with you if you don't have any.

☞Henny Youngman

---

718 Aunt Petley tells Uncle Slink that money can't buy friendship. He says, "Any friend that can't be bought ain't worth having in the first place."

---

719 Among the things that money can't buy is what it used to.

☞Max Kauffmann

---

720 My Uncle Crimel is a good example of gluttony. He enjoys eating so doggone much. And he's going to enjoy it even more once he discovers chewing.

---

721 Uncle Crimel not only has the appetite of an alligator, but also the table manners of one, too.

722 Uncle Crimel eats so fast that both his upper and lower lip have whiplash.

723 Uncle Crimel's teeth just keep on chewing and chewing ... even when they're in the glass by his bed.

724 Fang says he eats a lot to settle his nerves. I asked, "Have you seen where they're settling?"

☞Phyllis Diller

725 My favorite meal is breakfast, lunch, dinner, and in-between.

☞Totie Fields

726 Her favorite food is seconds.

☞Joan Rivers

727 He writes so well he makes me feel like putting my quill back in the goose.

☞Fred Allen

728 Envy is one of the Seven Deadly Sins I wish I had.

729 I asked my Uncle Willie what "Thou shalt not covet." meant. He said, "I don't know. I never looked it up in the dictionary for fear I might be doing it."

730 Anger is one of the Seven Deadly Sins and Uncle Grinch says that really makes him mad.

731 Uncle Grinch says there is such a thing as righteous anger. He says, "Righteous anger is what I have when some other fella gets me ticked off."

732 Uncle Grinch has a terrible temper. He even gets angry that there are six other Deadly Sins.

733 It takes a long time to lose my temper, but once lost I could not find it with a dog.

☞Mark Twain

STRICT UPBRINGING

734 My upbringing was very strict. Mom would never let me hang around with unsavory characters. I hardly got to know my brothers.

---

735 My mother didn't raise any "bad" kids. She gave us two choices — we could be good or we could be better.

---

736 My mom was very old-fashioned. My sister had to cry and plead to get a training bra. Even then, her husband had to go with her to buy it.

---

737 My parents were very strict. The Golden Rule in our house was "Do unto others as you would have them do unto you or Mom and Dad will do unto you something you wouldn't want done unto anybody."

---

738 Mom's philosophy was "Spare the rod and spoil the child." It wasn't so much a philosophy as it was a plan of attack.

739 Dad brought me behind the woodshed so many times that I began to build up Frequent Traveler mileage.

740 Americans are very religious people. You can tell by the way they drive.

☞Mark Twain

741 My mom and dad were very strict. In our household, the Ten Commandments were only the beginning.

742 Dad wanted his kids to be upstanding citizens. We were upstanding a lot, because we were too sore to sit down.

743 Living in our house was just like living in a church. We not only prayed a lot, we also took up collections.

744 Mom taught us that clean living was good for us. She said, "Your Uncle

Lemkin never smoked, never drank, and never ran around with women and this year he's going to celebrate his 92nd birthday."

My brother asked, "How?"

---

745 My mom was a strict disciplinarian. When she'd say, "Wait till your father gets home," it meant she was letting us off lightly.

---

746 There was never a hint of alcohol in our house — except when Uncle Filmur burped.

---

747 I was raised in the strict Jewish tradition, taught never to marry a Gentile woman, shave on Saturday and, most especially, never to shave a Gentile woman on Saturday.

☞Woody Allen

SUNDAY-GO-TO-MEETING CLOTHES

748 My mom always made me wear fresh undergarments to church. She said, "The Good Lord can see into your soul and He'll probably pass your underwear along the way."

749 Everybody wore their Sunday best at our church. In fact, I think some people showed up for services just because they'd bought the suit and didn't want to waste the money.

750 Any Sunday could be as popular as Easter at church if you called 'em fashion shows.

☞Will Rogers

751 A well-tied tie is the first serious step in life.

☞Oscar Wilde

752 I wore the same suit to church every Sunday for 13 years. I was always afraid I might die during the week, go to Heaven in my old clothes, and God wouldn't recognize me.

I wore that suit to services so often that if I couldn't make it on Sunday, that suit would go to church and sing all the hymns without me.

---

753 I may have worn the same suit too many times to services. I prayed for my daily bread and a voice from above said, "Would you mind if I throw in a new suit, too?"

---

754 My grandfather was a smart dresser. He invented spats. Well, he didn't exactly invent them — he just used to let his long underwear hang over his shoes.

☞Bob Hope

---

755 Us kids used to bet whether Mom was going to wear her best hat or her funniest hat. It was the same hat.

---

756 Her hat is a creation that will never go out of style. It will look just as ridiculous year after year.

☞Fred Allen

757 Momma had a Sunday hat that had so many flowers on it that she looked like a travelling funeral.

If Momma put wheels on that thing it could have been a float in the Fourth of July parade.

758 I always got spruced up to go to Sunday services. It made me wonder — what do atheists ever get dressed up for?

759 My mom asked me, "Did you wash behind your ears for church?" I said, "No, but if we sit in the last pew nobody'll notice."

...I stood for the entire service that Sunday — and prayed that I'd be able to sit down by the following Sunday.

ON WEARING YOUR SUNDAY BEST

760 Where lipstick is concerned, the important thing is not the color, but to accept God's final decision on where your lips end.

☞Jerry Seinfeld

761 Never let a panty line show around your ankles.

☞Joan Rivers

762 A clean tie always attracts the soup of the day.

☞Milton Berle

763 Be careless in your dress if you must, but keep a tidy soul.

☞Mark Twain

SUNDAY SCHOOL

764 On a clear and balmy weekend, Sunday school should be considered cruel and unusual education.

765 As a kid, my behind used to get sore from sitting in Sunday school. And if I played hookey, Dad made sure my behind would get sore from not sitting in Sunday school.

766 In Sunday school I learned there were many miracles in the Bible. For instance, it's a miracle that those people in the Old Testament ever learned to spell their own names.

767 In Sunday school I learned that Jonah spent three days in the belly of the whale — and this was in the days before Dramamine.

768 I first learned about Hell from my Sunday school teacher. She said if I didn't behave myself she'd knock it out of me.

769 Going to Sunday school is hereditary. If your mom and dad had to do it when they were young, they're going to make sure you have to do it, too.

770 Joshua brought down the walls of Jericho. Samson brought down the temple. In the Old Testament days they sure could have used better building inspectors.

771 Going to Sunday school always confused me. I had to wear my new clothes to study the Old Testament.

772 The Bible would be a lot different if I had been St. Paul. I would have written to places that were easier to spell.

If the Ephesians wanted to hear from me, they would all have to move to Ohio.

773 I always liked Sunday school when we studied the story of David and Goliath. I'd win a lot of money by betting the new kids on who was going to win.

SWEARING

774 Some guy hit my fender, and I said to him, "Be fruitful and multiply," but not in those words.

☞Woody Allen

775 Let us swear while we may, for in Heaven it will not be allowed.

☞Mark Twain

776 When my Uncle Fleebo starts swearing he could make a lobster blush.

777 Uncle Fleebo was the Roget's Thesaurus of swear words.

778 Uncle Fleebo was a master. He's the only man I ever knew who could cuss in the plus perfect pejorative.

779 When Uncle Fleebo let loose you had to consult a dictionary to find out if he was really swearing or not.
   ...He was.

780 My Uncle Fleebo has a colorful vocabulary. I've been to Thanksgiving dinners where he made the turkey blush.

781 He knows more four-letter words than the dictionary does.

782 Uncle Fleebo's vocabulary is so hot he can heat up your coffee with just a few well chosen phrases.

783 You can always spot Uncle Fleebo in a crowd. He the one with the blue cloud hanging over his head.

784 If you take Uncle Fleebo's bad words away from him, he's a mute.

785 When angry, count four; when very angry, swear.

☞Mark Twain

786 When Uncle Fleebo got angry he would count to ten, but every number had a few choice expletives in front of it.

787 Uncle Fleebo was famous for his swearing. Once our preacher accidentally banged his thumb with a hammer. The preacher couldn't swear, of course, so he went to Uncle Fleebo and said, "Would you say a few words over my thumb?"

---

788 Under certain circumstances, profanity provides a relief denied even to prayer.

☞Mark Twain

---

789 My mom didn't like swearing. She'd tell me, "One cuss word could send you to Hell. Two cuss words and I'll see to it that you make the trip today."

---

790 My mom would wash my mouth out with soap if she caught me swearing. For awhile there I had the foulest mouth and the cleanest tongue in the whole school.

I can taste those washings to this day. In fact, when I go to a fancy restaurant, I still ask for a wine that goes well with Ivory soap.

---

791 Swearing was invented as a compromise between running away and fighting.

☞Finley Peter Dunne

TEMPTATION

792 Temptation comes easy. Opportunity takes a little longer.

☞Milton Berle

---

793 Some people resist temptation because they're holy; others because they're cheap.

---

794 Resisting temptation is not only the right thing to do, but oftentimes it's the least expensive, too.

---

795 I generally avoid temptation unless I can't resist it.

☞Mae West

---

796 Temptation is a test to see if you're good enough. It's just like your driver's exam, except with temptation you don't have to wait in line as long.

---

797 Temptation gets easier as you get older. That's because there are fewer sins that you have the energy to commit.

798 My Uncle Fred says it's easy for him to resist temptation because there's no sins appealing enough for him to get out of his rocking chair.

799 Uncle Fred says if he wants to give in to temptation now, he needs a note from his doctor.

800 There are several good protections against temptation, but the surest is cowardice.

☞Mark Twain

801 My Uncle Willie often gives in to temptation — or anything else that's available.

802 Uncle Willie enjoys temptation so much he'll often drive four or five miles out of his way to find some.

803 The only time Uncle Willie doesn't give in to temptation is when he forgets to bring along enough cash.

804 Uncle Willie says he gives in to temptation because there's not much else he knows of that's as much fun to give in to.

805 Uncle Willie says that temptation comes in many different forms — half-pint, pint, fifth...

806 Uncle Willie gives in to temptation quite a bit. You've heard of the wages of sin? Uncle Willie gets a ten percent discount.

807 Aunt Gert says the only time Uncle Willie ever said, "Get thee behind me, Satan" was when he was in line waiting to get into the burlesque show.

808 Uncle Willie says if he gives up temptation he won't have any hobbies left.

809 Uncle Willie says that temptation is the welcome mat to sin ... and Aunt

Gert wants to know what Uncle Willie was doing on that doorstep in the first place.

---

810 When my dad was tempted by sweets, he'd say: "Well, if I finish these off, I won't be tempted anymore."

---

811 I can resist everything except temptation.

☞Oscar Wilde

---

812 Lead me not into temptation — I can find the way myself.

☞Rita Mae Brown

---

813 You show me a person who is no longer tempted, and I'll show you a person who's accompanied by six pallbearers.

---

814 Our preacher said in his sermon, in no uncertain terms, that we had to resist temptation. So I did. I was tempted to put five bucks in the collection, but instead I only put in a dollar.

TEN COMMANDMENTS

815 There are about ten million laws on the books all trying to enforce the The Ten Commandments.

☞Sam Levenson

---

816 Grandma used to say we had no choice but to be good. She said, "That's why God called them 'The Ten Commandments' and not 'The Ten Suggestions.' "

---

817 My Uncle Kram is a good man, but he's a slob. He should be grateful that the Good Lord only gave us Ten Commandments and not a dress code.

---

818 Uncle Tarn says he always observes the Ten Commandments — five a week for two weeks at a time.

---

819 Uncle Tarn says the Good Lord was pretty clever when He came up with those "shalt nots." He says, "They pretty much took care of most of my 'shalts.'"

---

820 Uncle Tarn has studied the Ten Commandments for years — looking for loopholes.

---

821 Uncle Tarn says we don't have to be too worried about keeping the Ten Commandments. "After all," he says, "They're not carved in stone, you know."

---

822 Uncle Tarn admits he's not so good at keeping the Ten Commandments. He says the only chance he has of getting to Heaven is if the Good Lord grades on a curve.

---

823 Uncle Tarn says if the Good Lord was serious about the Ten Commandments, He would have added an eleventh one that says, "Thou shalt keep the first ten."

---

824 Aunt Reedley says the Good Lord was serious. That's why they say "Thou shalt not..." rather than "Don't you think it would be a good idea if..."

---

825 When you think about it, ten Commandments are not so bad. I have more chores than that to do before I go to school each morning.

---

826 Say what you will about the Ten Commandments, you always come back to the pleasant fact that there are only ten of them.

☞H. L. Mencken

---

827 You can get into Heaven by obeying just ten commandments, but I had to sign a 62-page agreement to get into my condominium.

---

828 Have you ever noticed? There are ten Commandments and only seven deadly sins. It seems like the odds favor the house.

829 Some people feel things might have been easier if God gave us ten Commandments — pick any three.

830 My Aunt Maritta is so saintly she tries to keep eleven Commandments.
   ...She's keeping one for extra credit.

831 This lady wanted to mail a Bible to her son at college. The post office clerk wanted to know if the package contained anything breakable.
   "Only the Ten Commandments," she replied.

☞ Joey Adams

UNSELFISHNESS

832 My mother always told me, "Bring enough for everybody." When I was drafted, I showed up with six duffel bags full of chewing gum ... khaki flavored.

833 Mom tried to teach us kids to be unselfish, but it was hard. As a youngster, the only thing I willingly shared with my brother was the trouble I got into.

He was certainly welcome to more than half of that.

---

834 If there were two biscuits on the table I would wrestle with my conscience whether to take the bigger one or the smaller. While I was doing that, my brother would eat both of them.

---

835 Once my mother was going shopping and I said, "Get me a toy." My mom got annoyed and said, "Get me ... get me ... get me — don't you ever think about giving?" I said, "Sure I do. After you get me the toy, I want you to give it to me."

---

836 My mom told us we should always give more than we get. With that one sentence she seems to have summed up all of my tax returns.

---

837 The only thing we did share was clothes. I even wore hand-me-down diapers. When I got diaper rash, my older brother scratched.

---

838 The first time I had clothes of my own, my wife had to come and help me buy them.

---

839 By the time I got new clothes, the seat of the old pants was worn so thin I could sit on a dime and tell you if it was heads or tails.

Some of them were worn even thinner. I could sit on a dollar bill and tell you if it was heads or tails ... and if George Washington had shaved that morning or not.

---

840 Everyone knew I wore hand-me-downs. One time the fifth grade teacher yelled at me, "The last time those clothes were in this grade, they behaved much better."

---

841 I got used to hand-me-downs. Once I got a bad rash and Mom said, "Why didn't you tell me about this sooner?" I said, "To tell you the truth, Mom, I wasn't sure this was my skin."

---

842 I was even married in one of my brother's hand-me-down suits. After the ceremony I went on my honeymoon, but the suit was arrested for bigamy.

VIRTUE

843 Search others for their virtues, thyself for thy vices.

☞Ben Franklin

---

844 Some people claim to be virtuous when all they really are is lazy.

---

845 In our world today, virtue has become like football, baseball, and basketball — primarily a spectator sport.

---

846 There's one good thing about growing older — virtue becomes easier.

847 Virtue is its own reward. It has to be. There's no point in being good for prizes. You have to be good for nothing.

848 Virtue has its own reward — but has no sale at the box office.

☞Mae West

849 To be worth anything, virtue must be more than the lack of opportunity.

850 Virtue is a lot like playing the harmonica. A lot of people are not as good at it as they think they are.

851 Virtue is very delicate. It's the art of having a good quality without being obnoxious about it.

852 I knew one person who said he had so many virtues he couldn't imagine what others he could have. I suggested humility.

853 Virtue is like a tattoo. If you don't have it all the time, it isn't real.

854 I knew one gentleman who wore all of his virtues proudly, like a uniform. He also took a lot of them off at night.

WALKING ON WATER

855 I wish I could walk on water. I wouldn't flaunt it, but I would take a few strokes off my golf game ... and save a fortune in golf balls.

856 A little advice — if you're going to try to walk on water, learn to swim first.

857 I have a friend who actually can walk on water. Of course, his feet are shaped like pontoons.

858 It's good that only a select few can walk on water. Why put all those bridge builders out of work?

859 You show me a person who thinks he can walk on water and I'll show you a person who's going to spend a lot of time reaching for life preservers ... and wringing out wet underwear.

860 There's not much advantage to walking on water anyway — unless you're the type of person who likes to jog on Lake Erie. ... or would enjoy hiking to England. ... or are a street walker in Venice.

861 I've known quite a few people who thought they could walk on water. I've given artificial respiration to number of them.

862 I really believe I can walk on water. In fact, I've had the surface of my swimming pool carpeted.

863 Not only can I not walk on water, I can't even hit a golf ball over it.

864 I really can walk on water though ... if it's cold enough.

865 My Uncle Clydorf thinks he can walk on water, but the truth is, on weekends he often has trouble walking on dry land.

866 Anyone can walk on water if they truly believe they can — and know where the underwater rocks are.

...WHO HELP THEMSELVES

867 The Lord helps those who help themselves. When I was a kid I learned that at our house the Lord better help anyone who helps himself before Mom said Grace.

868 He's a self-made man. Nobody else was willing to take the blame for it.

869 He's a self-made man ... the living proof of the horrors of unskilled labor.

☞Ed Wynn

870 I'm a self-made man; who else would help?

☞Oscar Levant

871 I'm a terrible do-it-yourselfer. I've got our plumbing so messed up now that we have to get our water by mail.

872 I was a little optimistic when I installed the VCR by myself. Now I get movies on my electric can opener.

☞Milton Berle

873 I have bad luck fixing mechanical things. I have a clock that runs counterclockwise.

☞Woody Allen

874 My Uncle Gerwalt used to say, "The best place to find a helping hand is at the end of your arm." He checked the end of his arm one day and found out someone had helped themselves to his watch.

875 Uncle Wolfer always said he was a self-made man and I believed him. He didn't look like the work of a professional.

876 My mom always said, "If you want something done, do it yourself" — then she'd assign our chores.

877 I have a new book coming out. It's one of those self-help deals. It's called *"How to Get Along with Everybody."* I wrote it with some other jerk.

☞Steve Martin

878 "God helps those who help themselves" — that's the national motto for the Shoplifter Society of America.

879 My Uncle Felmark always said, "The best place to find a helping hand is at the end of your arm." His son, Gerdal, believed it — he became a pickpocket.

880 I find the trouble with being a self-made man is that it's so hard to get replacement parts.

881 Good advice is to pray as if everything depended on God, but work as if everything depended on you — and keep receipts as if everything depended on the IRS.

YOU CAN'T TAKE IT WITH YOU

882 The trouble is, if you don't use what Mother Nature gave you, Father Time will take it away.

☞Milton Berle

883 They say you can't take it with you. I'm having trouble getting enough to use while I'm here.

884 My Great Uncle Delbar was so cheap he lived to be 102 years old. He said, "If you can't take it with you, I ain't going until the last minute."

885 This idea that you can't take it with you may be a myth. Wouldn't it be terrible if we got to the Pearly Gates only to find out they're coin operated.

886 We suspect that's why Uncle Grimsley is so generous to the church. He knows you can't take it with you, so he's trying to send it on ahead.

887 My rich Uncle Dilby knows you can't take it with you, but he wants to be buried with an accountant just in case.

888 There is a saying — you can't take it with you — but if you see a funeral procession with a Brink's armored truck behind the hearse, you'll know Jack is having a try at it.

☞Fred Allen (about Jack Benny)

889 It's well known you can't take it with you. That's why you always see pictures of angels wearing wings and not money belts.

...And you never see angels wearing shoes. They've got no money to buy them.

---

890 You can't take it with you. The flight to Heaven allows no carry-on luggage.

---

891 You can't take it with you — yet another good reason why not too many people want to go just yet.

---

892 You won't need money in Heaven. Everything's included in the price of admission.

---

893 You can't take it with you, which probably means St. Peter doesn't make much on tips for opening the Pearly Gates.

---

894 Money is absolutely worthless in Heaven. With inflation, it's getting pretty close to that here, too.

---

895 You can't take it with you, which is good. It means there are no taxes in

Heaven … and if there are, you won't be able to afford them.

---

896 You won't have any money in the afterlife. I don't know about you, but that's not much different from the way I'm living now.

---

897 There will be no money problems in the afterlife. Is it any wonder they call it Heaven?

ZEBRAS

898 Why did God make striped horses? They were originally designed to be the referees at Polo matches.

---

899 One fellow in Africa chased down a zebra and made a coat for his brother in jail.

☞Milton Berle

---

900 Our village idiot bought himself a zebra. Named it "Spot."

☞Henny Youngman